Glamorous RETREATS

JAN SHOWERS

PHOTOGRAPHY BY JEFF MCNAMARA

ABRAMS, NEW YORK

EDITOR: REBECCA KAPLAN
DESIGNER: DEB WOOD
PRODUCTION MANAGER: TRUE SIMS

LIBRARY OF CONGRESS CONTROL NUMBER: 2013935887

ISBN: 978-1-4197-0853-4

PRINTED AND BOUND IN CHINA
10 9 8 7 6 5 4 3 2 1

ABRAMS BOOKS ARE AVAILABLE AT SPECIAL DISCOUNTS
WHEN PURCHASED IN QUANTITY FOR PREMIUMS
AND PROMOTIONS AS WELL AS FUNDRAISING OR
EDUCATIONAL USE. SPECIAL EDITIONS CAN ALSO BE
CREATED TO SPECIFICATION. FOR DETAILS, CONTACT
SPECIALSALES@ABRAMSBOOKS.COM OR THE ADDRESS BELOW.

ABRAMS
THE ART OF BOOKS SINCE 1949

115 WEST 18TH STREET
NEW YORK, NY 10011
WWW.ABRAMSBOOKS.COM

TO JIM,

MY PARTNER

IN EVERYTHING

I DO.

Contents

Introduction

RETREATS ARE OTHER WORLDS, SET APART
FROM OUR EVERYDAY LIVES. THE HOUSES IN
THESE PAGES ARE PLACES WHERE MY CLIENTS
GO TO EXPERIENCE LIFE IN ALL ITS RICHNESS
AND TO RECONNECT WITH SIMPLICITY,
NATURE, ART, PLEASURE, AND RELAXATION.

There are twelve projects in these pages. The design of each house is shaped by an understanding, not simply of style or aesthetic taste, but of the special circumstances and desires that make it attractive to its owners. A retreat isn't like a primary residence. My clients are drawn to them because of the way they feel in these unique and magical settings.

There are many considerations in designing a house based on location. A beach house requires a particular practical understanding, as does a ski lodge—these houses exist for a special purpose in a special place.

Then, of course, the views of the outdoors must be considered, since the enjoyment of the natural environment is often the purpose for these houses. With the views come the colors of nature, which are taken into account in almost every design decision. In the desert, sage greens, pale blues, and sand colors. Near the ocean, the striking azure of sea and sky. In the mountains, the white of snow in winter and the green of fir trees.

The climate informs another set of decisions that can be described in one word: "appropriateness," or what Elsie de Wolfe called "suitability." I would never use velvet or mohair in a summer home. And I would never put an animal print rug on the floor of a beach house.

NANTUCKET

Brant Point Seaside Cottage

When Carla and Jack McDonald moved from New York to Austin, Texas, for business reasons, they planned to return to New York after a few years, but they quickly fell in love with the idiosyncratic capital city and became deeply involved with its entrepreneurial, cultural, and philanthropic scene. As we were completing design work on their first Austin house, they were already looking for a permanent home for their family. The magnificent French limestone house they selected is a favorite project of mine, and one I featured prominently in my first book, *Glamorous Rooms*. When Carla called to tell me about the Nantucket cottage they were building with architect Milton Rowland, I knew we would have another fun collaboration, because we had worked so well together on their Austin properties.

The McDonalds have been summering in Nantucket as a family for more than a decade, returning to the place Carla visited and loved as a child. Jack is a novice sailor, having spent the last few summers sailing a Rhodes 19, and both Carla and Jack enjoy playing golf and tennis. Their daughters, Ava and Devin, have grown up looking forward to charmed summers on the island.

Their beach house, in the Cliffside area of Brant Point, is a classic Nantucket shingle-style cottage, with a stunning interior that is far from typical. Carla has great style and is quite glamorous, which played into every decision as we undertook the design. Whenever possible, we steered clear of standard beach house decor, opting instead for refined colors, textures, materials, and art. However, we were always careful to keep the decor appropriate to Nantucket.

The living space off the entry has a sophisticated, inviting vibe. The wool rug, the book-lined shelves, and the fireplace all create an intimate and inviting atmosphere, in any season. I particularly love the custom-size blue, sea grass, and ivory rug. It was the starting point for all the fabrics and textures in the room. We used a pair of faux-bamboo wing chairs, which we found in a vintage shop and thought looked "very Nantucket" in the best possible sense. The upholstery is a wonderful sea-motif toile in blues and greens. Handsome hand-thrown ceramic lamps from the 1950s lend the room a brilliant, watery iridescence. In the corner, a raffia-upholstered Louis XVI-style bergère and ottoman create an ideal spot for reading by the fire.

Though I found the bronze and glass coffee table in Paris on a buying trip months earlier, it finally arrived just a day or two before Carla and Jack came to my showroom to make selections. Kismet inevitably plays a tremendous role in every design. It was so serendipitous that the McDonalds arrived when they did. The table is a chic addition that transforms the room, adding character as all coffee tables should, but also bringing an element of glamour to the space.

As for the art over the fireplace, Carla, who is always game for unexpected choices, selected Slim Aarons' photograph, titled *Poolside Gossip*, rather than the usual sand-and-sea scenes. Aarons' photography can be found throughout the house, in fact. Carla treasures her vintage copy of Slim Aarons' *A Wonderful Time*, which has a place of honor on the coffee table.

The dining room is adjacent to the living room, and we made the decision not to use a rug, in part because it is a high-traffic area, but mostly because we all loved the warm look of the exposed wood floors. The dining room is very carefully edited. An unusually wide, almost square French mirror expands the visual space and adds depth to the room. It reflects the turquoise Elizabeth Chandelier, which is so unexpected in a Nantucket house. Six antique ivory painted Coco chairs from my furniture collection are upholstered in azure faux patent leather. The chair backs are upholstered in raffia, giving them a pleasantly casual air.

Passing through the central living space one arrives in a charming, very open sunporch with a sofa and a pair of wonderful vintage French rattan-and-wicker lounge chairs. Carla has a writing desk at one end of the sunporch, a delightful place to use her computer and write notes and letters.

Upstairs, the master suite has a vaulted attic ceiling and is painted in Benjamin Moore Yarmouth Blue. We hung a white glass chandelier in the middle of the room, as I always recommend when working with high ceilings.

The second floor sitting room has some of the best ocean views in the house and serves as the main hangout for the family, where they can watch TV or just take in the view.

Ava and Devin share a bedroom just down the hall. The girls wanted their room to express what summer on Nantucket means to them, eating ice cream and searching for seashells. Many of the shells they've collected are displayed throughout the house, a playful reminder of summers past and summers to come in their seaside retreat.

PRECEDING PAGES:

Poolside Gossip by Slim Aarons hangs above the fireplace and helps create a relaxed tone for this living space. The wing chairs are upholstered in Pindler Seward in Seaspray. A favorite find in Paris, the 1970s bronze coffee table helps pull the room together.

ABOVE:

Hand-thrown vintage iridescent ceramic lamps flank the living room sofa.

OPPOSITE:

The sparkling glass accessories, paired with the rug, suggest the colors of the sea.

ABOVE AND OPPOSITE:
A glamorous Louis XVI-style
table from the 1940s combined
with Coco Chairs upholstered
in faux patent leather with raffia
backs. The Elizabeth Chandelier
in turquoise creates visual
impact when reflected in the
oversized French 1930s mirror.

LEFT:
A simple light-colored
kitchen is the perfect touch
for a beach house.

A classic Nantucket sunporch
with vintage French rattan-and-
wicker chairs.

A strong geometric pattern
on the bedding and Benjamin
Moore Wythe Blue wall color
create a soothing palette for
the master bedroom.

OPPOSITE:
The upstairs sitting room is
filled with whimsical color
combinations of tangerine
and peridot that allow white
elements to pop.

ABOVE:
The bedroom shared by the
girls is a playful escape.

SHANNON AND TED SKOKOS PAVILION

N. Pearl St.

NEIMAN

FORTY FIVE TEN

Nasher Sculpture Center

DALLAS

Up in the Air

Bob and Myrna Schlegel are well-known philanthropists who are prominent on the Dallas social scene. They have long been active with the city's cultural institutions, particularly the Dallas Symphony Orchestra, for which Myrna served as president. The family loves their large Preston Hollow estate, where they have entertained innumerable guests from all over the world, but when the W Dallas Victory Hotel and Residences broke ground, they saw an opportunity to have something completely different. They didn't want to replace their estate but rather to have an alternative urban getaway, a place where they could entertain near the city's sporting and cultural centers.

Before construction was complete, they purchased the entire twenty-ninth floor of the W Residences, with more than 11,000 square feet of interior space and some of the most spectacular, soaring views anywhere in Dallas. Lionel Morrison of Morrison Dilworth + Walls was hired as the architect.

The Schlegels have four children: Kim, Kari, Kirby, and Krystal. I have known them all for years and have done several projects with Kim and her husband, Justin Whitman. Their house appeared in my first book. I was very pleased to get the call to work with Bob and Myrna on their downtown property.

It was decided at the start that the central area of the twenty-ninth floor would be made into an entertainment space with a massive bar for hosting large groups. This would leave two equal units on either side of approximately 5,000 square feet each, where Kari, a graduate student, and Kirby, a sports team owner, would each have their own residences.

Kari has a very definite style. I had worked with her previously on a condominium project, so we had already established a shared language. She had a vision from the start. Because she loves color and combining color with white, that became a common thread throughout her space. Kari found a lot of interesting pieces on her own, discovering, for example, a vivid amethyst chandelier in Los Angeles to go with the yellow satin Louis XVI–style chairs I'd found in Paris. The combination of purple and yellow is so Kari and added exactly the right punch to the space.

The most important thing to Kari was the city views. The architecture revolves around them, and so did the design. The loft-like interior has few walls, and windows everywhere, so we focused on using low-profile, light, and—in the case of a Lucite dining table—transparent furniture.

One of my favorite things about working with Kari is her complete fearlessness about mixing old and new. She's never reluctant when it comes to blending styles and periods. In her entry hall, we used an eighteenth-century piano, a nineteenth-century Napoleon III mirror, twentieth-century Louis XV–style chairs from the Eden Roc Hotel, and a 1950s clear Murano chandelier. They work together in such a smart and unexpected way. I've said before that the entry sets the tone for the house, and nowhere is that more evident than here.

The views made her bedroom one of the biggest challenges of all. There are two walls that are not glass—one of which definitely could not accommodate a bed. The other wall was the obvious choice for the bed, but it didn't allow for the best view of the city, which Kari wanted to see upon waking in the morning. That view was nonnegotiable as far as she was concerned, so we fabricated the headboard itself as a wall in the corner. On the opposite side of the room, we created a matching upholstered corner wall, which contains a seating area.

One of my favorite color combinations is Benjamin Moore's Palladian Blue mixed with almost any green. So the headboard and seating walls were made of a silk in that color, accented with green lamps on either side of the bed and a chic green chair in the sitting area.

"Spa-like" is a term so ubiquitous that it's almost meaningless, but in Kari's bath, it couldn't be more accurate. The room truly is like a spa in the sky.

Jack, Kari's miniature Pinscher, was the love of her life until she met her husband, Troy Kloewer—but Jack still runs the show on the twenty-ninth floor of the W.

On Kirby's side of the retreat, sports reign. He is an avid fan who loves sports memorabilia and comfortable seating for watching games on TV. He's very tactile and sensitive to texture. In designing the space, we had to be certain that every fabric, carpet, and rug passed the Kirby touch test.

Most people imagine retreats in ocean or mountain settings, but the Schlegels' is twenty-nine stories in the sky in the middle of one of the most exciting cities in the world.

A lounge area in the party
room is reminiscent of El
Morocco, a famous Manhattan
nightclub from the 1930s to the
1950s.

The spectacular sycamore bar,
designed by Morrison Dilworth
+ Walls, is the centerpiece of
the entertainment space.

KARI

OPPOSITE:
Lemon-yellow satin chairs from
the Eden Roc Hotel flank a
nineteenth-century mirror.

ABOVE:
A graphic black-and-white Ellipse
Rug from Stark mimics the zebra
in the entryway. Citrine-colored
Murano lamps flank the Villa Sofa.
Vintage chairs from the 1950s
perfectly pair with the Sabine
Coffee Table.

OPPOSITE:
In a casual seating and dining
area, lemon yellow makes
another appearance with the
addition of a vivid amethyst
chandelier. Louis XVI–style
chairs surround an Oliver
dining table. Custom rug is
by Stark.

ABOVE:
We designed this mirrored bar, which is as functional as it is glamorous.

OPPOSITE:
A Lucite game table with priceless Dallas views. Chairs are Opera One by Pierantonio Bonacin.

Kari's bedroom is designed to capture the views. On display, one of my favorite color combinations: robin's egg blue and lime green. The Audrey Slipper Chair faces the baker's coffee table and custom banquette.

ABOVE AND OPPOSITE:
Kari's spa-like bath. Her closet
and bath have spectacular
views of the city.

KIRBY

Kirby, a huge sports fan who was very involved with his family's sports team, wanted his place to be masculine and comfortable. He wanted the design to be geared around TVs for viewing sporting events, and he made clear his desire to have lots of space dedicated to entertaining.

We designed a custom burled rosewood dining table that sits in the middle of a large combination living/dining room. His sister Kim contributed an unexpected element to the room—a set of chrome mid-century dining chairs she bought from the Tom Landry estate, knowing her brother's love for the Dallas Cowboys.

I have never before used an antler chandelier, but I couldn't think of anything more fabulous and fun in this sleek setting. This one, found in Santa Fe, creates a sculpture above the table.

Although the palette is neutral and masculine—we even upholstered the long, low sofas in a wool worsted pinstripe flannel—Kirby's personality is everywhere, particularly in the art and accessories.

ABOVE:
Kirby's living area with Barcelona chair and chaise is great for entertaining, as well as relaxing at home.

RIGHT:
An unexpected antler chandelier hangs above the sleek dining table.

Kirby's bedroom is my favorite room in his residence. It's very large yet has a warm, intimate feel because of the two seating areas on either side of the room, each very different from the other. On one end, a Platner Table is accessorized with stacks of books and an interesting antique globe. On the opposite end, a thick shag carpet anchors black-and-white upholstered cowhide chaises in front of a late-Deco rosewood French credenza.

On either side of the bed, Miles Mineral Lamps from my collection serve as a handsome accent against the background of walls painted a dark slate blue. The drapery, in the same color, is wool limousine cloth.

OPPOSITE:
A Texas cowhide chaise
juxtaposed against a late
1930s French rosewood
credenza.

ABOVE:
Kirby's bedroom is a dark,
masculine space with luxurious
limousine cloth drapery and
a pair of Miles Mineral Lamps
made of honeycomb calcite.

OPPOSITE:
A Platner Table holds interesting
books and objects as well as a
favorite globe.

BACHELOR GULCH

OPPOSITE:
Loius XVI–style leather fauteuils and a nickle chandelier lend a rich, glamorous feel to this lodge.

ABOVE:
A nineteenth-century alabaster chandelier hangs over an antique table with a mix of glass, ceramic, and modern accessories.

ABOVE:

Interesting vintage wood and metal lamps sit on a nineteenth-century French pine buffet.

OPPOSITE:

A late 1930s French game table and chairs with vintage amber glass are situated to capture the views.

In the master bedroom an iron
bed is hung with Italian voile
drapery. The chandelier is from
the Arts and Crafts period.

A pitch pine French armoire from
the late nineteenth century is
flanked by framed herbiers of the
same era.

ABOVE:

A French writing desk sits in the corner of the master bedroom.

OPPOSITE:

Louis XVI bergères frame the gorgeous views from the master suite. Mohair from Clarence House.

Spectacular outdoor living
with French garden furniture.

TORONTO

Art House

Cecily and Robert Bradshaw live in Toronto, where Robert paints and sculpts and Cecily, a devoted equestrian, rides dressage. Together, they are passionate art collectors with a refined interest in contemporary art. When they met, Robert was living in Rosedale, a fashionable district of Toronto, in what he referred to as a "bachelor pad"—a handsome house overlooking one of the city's famous ravines. After they married, they realized that there was insufficient space to display their ever-growing collection of art and sculpture. When a large piece of property next door to the existing house became available, they jumped at the opportunity to purchase it. Architect Wayne Swadron was brought on to design what the Bradshaws refer to, somewhat modestly, as the Guest House. It's true that the new space provides additional bedrooms for family and friends. However, a much larger area is devoted to housing and displaying their substantial art collection in a space that can also be used for entertaining friends and the many cultural groups with which they are associated, including local art museums and the symphony.

The Bradshaws contacted me after construction was complete on the Guest House. Cecily had read my first book, *Glamorous Rooms*, and found she related to my aesthetic. I flew to Toronto for our first meeting and was impressed with both properties—the original and the Guest House—but there was a great deal of work to be done. The entire process took more than a year.

The Guest House is composed of three floors. The entrance is on the second floor. When I first saw the house, the entry hall was a combination of natural-colored wood and upholstered walls that did not enhance the beauty of the surrounding rooms, the black-and-white stone floor, or the stunning black lacquered staircase visible in the next room. I felt strongly that the walls and ceilings needed to be lacquered black for dramatic effect, and to set off the beauty of the galleries on either side. I presented the idea during a phone conversation, and the Bradshaws were open but wanted to see a rendering and have a section of the room painted as a test. A black panel was lacquered and hung in the entry, and the rendering was completed, upon which they were fully on board. The results are splendid.

Cecily had a vision of what she wanted in the entry hall. She imagined a pair of intricately carved, gilded mirrors, hung almost as art objects. We searched for antique mirrors in the proper scale and style to no avail. Finally, we had the mirrors hand carved and gilded in Dallas, in the perfect style and scale. Custom demilunes were fabricated, upon which gold Murano lamps found in Paris light the scene and create a reflective glow.

To the right of the entry hall is the salon, which contains both art and sculpture, and two seating areas flank the fireplace. The iconic, sculptural René Drouet gilded iron and mirrored coffee tables are the centerpieces of the seating areas. We used Cecily's favorite colors: Kyle Bunting cowhide in mint on Louis XV–style chairs, with pale sky-blue silk on the Palm Beach Banquettes. Above, geometric editions by Jason Salavon and Capri Floor Lamps in gold Murano glass complete the scene.

To the left of the entry is the Gallery. A grand piano sits in the corner, as this room is used for very large seated dinners and parties. Guests are surrounded by works of art by Peter Kolisnyk and Ross Bleckner. We made four custom Lindsay Benches from which to enjoy the works on display when the Bradshaws are not entertaining.

Down the black staircase, the first floor is also filled with art and sculpture— including a stunning work by Massimo Listri, a very appropriate photograph that captures the interior of another gallery. Nearby, a painting by Robert lends the space a graphic and dramatic atmosphere. Those works flank the door to the library, a book-lined room with a Kyle Bunting ivory cowhide rug I designed called Moonglow. Cecily and Robert enjoy entertaining friends and often turn the large library table into a dining space for six to eight.

The master suite, on the third floor, has a private terrace that overlooks a sculpture garden. Bronze and glass rod lamps from the 1970s flank the bed on late Deco–style commodes. A luxuriously deep settee sits at the end of the bed, paired with a Baxter Coffee Table from my collection, and a Murano chandelier from the 1940s hangs above.

The Bradshaws' main residence

The garden, designed by landscape architect Tina McMullen, has a tremendous variety of intriguing, carefully curated sculpture on display, including works by Robert. There, Cecily and Robert enjoy art and the outdoors with their beloved King Charles spaniel, Mr. Dickens. It's no exaggeration to say that it is a magical, otherworldly place—precisely as the Bradshaws intended.

OPPOSITE:
The Guest House.

ABOVE:
Robert and Cecily enjoy late
afternoons in the loggia. All
furniture by McKinnon & Harris;
outdoor lamp by Live.Well.

PRECEDING PAGES:
The black laquered foyer
provides a dramatic entrance
as well as contrasting with the
white galleries on either side.
The Sebastien Demilunes
and custom carved gold leaf
mirrors with gold Murano lamps
raise the glamour quotient.

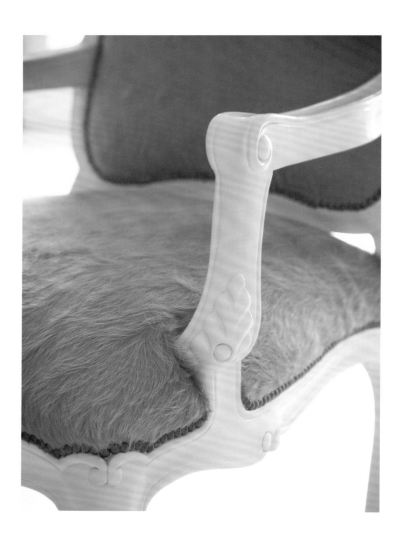

A pair of Palm Beach
banquettes and Marie Chairs
flank a fireplace in one of
the galleries, along with a pair
of Rene Drouet tea tables.

PRECEDING PAGES:
In the gallery, dramatic,
minimalist works by Peter
Kolisnyk.

LEFT:
A massive Massimo Listri work
in the downstairs gallery
leading to the library, with a
work by Robert Bradshaw to the
left of the door.

PRECEDING PAGES:
Bookcases in this paneled library contain the Bradshaws' collection of art books. A Kyle Bunting rug called Moonglow lightens the space.

RIGHT:
The master bedroom has a view of the sculpture garden. The vintage Murano chandelier was found in Paris. All pillows are custom, and the 1970s lamps flanking the bed are bronze with glass rods.

Robert Bradshaw's work is
featured among the sculptures
in the sculpture garden.

Chic Beach Sanctuary

Patty Lowdon—a fellow Texan—has her primary residence in Fort Worth and spends her summers in Newport and her winters in Palm Beach. When she called to ask if I'd like to design her Palm Beach getaway, she said, "I love your glamorous touch." Of course it was right up my alley. The two of us worked together over the course of a year to achieve a look befitting Patty's style.

Patty is a very glamorous woman with a rich social life. Well-dressed and always perfectly put together, she is also a consummate traveler. One has the sense that Patty has just returned from somewhere fabulous or is leaving for a wonderful destination any day. And she is a true sportswoman, having played tennis professionally, winning a number of prestigious titles in both singles and doubles.

The first step in any design project is to interview clients about their specific preferences—colors, furniture styles, and other personal requirements. From the beginning, Patty expressed her preference for whites, blues, and platinums. And naturally, it was a given that we would coordinate everything with the amazing ocean views.

Most of the interiors of the house are painted white, with the exception of the bedrooms and a small sitting room. White creates such a light and cool background for ocean colors. It's soothing and sophisticated, which is precisely as it should be. The floor plan is very open, so the space seems to go on forever. The living and dining areas are one large room, beyond which you see the Florida room and then the ocean. It feels truly expansive and so dramatic when your eye reaches the sea.

We found a great mirrored console for the entry as well as an Italian mirror, and we used a pair of vintage lilac-blue Murano lamps and a Claudette Bench upholstered in Hinson Snow Leopard, which adds a smart, graphic element.

Patty is tall and slender, and she has a tall son and son-in-law, so this had to be taken into consideration when making seating choices. Some were custom additions, and others were existing pieces Patty asked us to use in the new design. The living room sofas and chaises are wide and long, so that people can recline and watch TV. We also added a charming overscaled Daniele Tête-à-Tête.

Patty has a very edited and refined collection of vintage Murano glass throughout the house, primarily in blues. Along with subtle touches of mirror here and there, the glass adds a dramatic sparkling quality to the space. The ocean and shimmering glass seem to go together. But then I love beautiful glass pieces in any setting.

A custom-designed dining table in bleached sycamore goes with Patty's existing dining chairs and the custom chandelier, which is one of a kind, made in Murano for her. A 1930s mirrored screen separates the kitchen and bar from the dining area.

I love Patty's sunroom. Well, anywhere else it would be called a sunroom, but in Palm Beach, everyone refers to them as Florida Rooms. These are casual spaces for playing cards and unwinding. It's my favorite place in the house. We used the same bright blue and white fabric on her existing ivory lacquered faux-bamboo chairs and sofa. It's very old-school to match the upholstery in that way, and so fitting for a Florida Room. I'm crazy about the results!

When it came to Patty's bedroom, we settled on platinum walls for a cool, soothing effect. After the selection of the wall color, it was agreed that the bedding, lamps, and night tables would all be white. A Mercer Bench upholstered in pale sky-blue faux suede with Lucite legs seems to float at the foot of the bed.

A fabulous white faux suede Carlton Chair and ottoman in the corner are done in reverse French welt, which adds detail. It looks so stylish, and it is exceedingly practical as an upholstery selection for a beach house.

Of course, in Palm Beach, outdoor living is a given, especially with Patty's ocean views. There is no place in her house more comfortable than the loggia, where, as in the rest of the house, the white walls complement her colorful, interesting art.

Palm Beach is a world unto itself, where one is never at a loss for things to do. It's a town filled with fun and interesting people, great food, and the best shopping anywhere on Worth Avenue. A truly glamorous retreat.

OPPOSITE:

A side loggia is perfect for afternoon drinks or morning coffee.

A Daniele Tête-à-Tête sits at one
end of the living room with the
Florida room and the ocean
beyond.

OPPOSITE:

A unique twenty-four-arm
Murano chandelier illuminates
a 1930s mirrored screen and
a Lombard Table in bleached
sycamore.

A small sitting room with Louis
XV-style fauteuils
and a daybed with a view of
the ocean.

PRECEDING PAGES:
The Florida Room is filled with vintage rattan furniture from the 1960s. All chairs and sofas are upholstered in Lulu DK Porcupine.

ABOVE AND OPPOSITE:
A needlepoint backgammon set, a Lucite drinks cart, and a striped cotton rug add splashes of green, turquoise, and pink to the room.

The master bedroom, with a
view to the ocean, is quiet and
serene. A Carlton Chair sits in
the corner.

CRESTED BUTTE

An antique ivory Chandler
Commode with trademark
white cowhide and a 1970s
bronze French mirror add light
and a reflective quality to
Sherri's office.

OPPOSITE:

Stairs lead up to the bedrooms. A crystal chandelier and nickel sconces light the way.

ABOVE:

Upstairs in the children's room, custom-designed bunk beds with drapery and reading lights are practical and attractive.

ABOVE:

The master bath and dressing room serve as an entry to the master suite. A vintage Murano lamp and chandelier illuminate the space.

OPPOSITE:

A 1940s French mirrored and merisier dressing table adds glamour to the master bath.

All walls, bedding, window treatments, and upholstery in the master bedroom are done in Brunschwig & Fils Bengali Toile. Yellow vintage Murano glass and lamp sit atop the 1940s French sycamore credenza.

A terrace off the master
bedroom with an iron and
hand-painted tile coffee table
from France, c. 1940.

OPPOSITE:
Bookcases flank the rock
fireplace, and an antique
French console sits in the
center of the room.

ABOVE:
A collection of amber vintage
glass complements an ancient
mosaic coffee table.

ABOVE:
An antique dinner bell sits near
the dining area.

OPPOSITE:
A rustic farm table with heavy
leather dining chairs and
a carved antique German
commode are featured in the
dining room along with an
Indonesian tapestry.

ABOVE:
A pair of English club chairs flanks a round English Regency table with a vintage Murano lamp in peridot.

OPPOSITE:
In the master suite, a Bennison Acorn linen and an antelope rug by Stark add warmth to the cozy bedroom.

FOLLOWING PAGES:
A loggia leading to a new master suite with bergères in buttercream velvet flanking an antique cerused oak demilune.

Little Bay

Susanna and Palmer Moldawer, my daughter and son-in-law, first went to Harbour Island 18 years ago when their oldest child was still a baby. All these years later, this island in the Bahamas remains a favorite place for them and their children, Matthew, Ben, and Eliza. The locale is more than just an ocean view for them. They love the island's rich history, the culture, the people, and the relaxed pace and atmosphere. Though her primary residence is in Houston, Susanna was raised in a small Texas town. The community of Harbour Island gives her an opportunity to recapture all she misses about small-town life, with the added benefit of a magical natural environment. Aside from the stunning vistas of blue waters, there are the beaches, which are famous for their crystalline sand with its unusual pink cast.

For five years, Susanna and Palmer rented Little Bay on the bay side of the island in an area known as The Narrows. It's easy to see why they keep going back to it. Particularly given the island's small size, their house feels very isolated and set apart. If they don't feel like taking their golf cart—as everyone on the island does—the beaches are a short stroll from their back door.

When Little Bay became available for sale three years ago, they bought it without hesitation. I knew it would be a fun project because Susanna and I had done her primary residence in Houston, and we've worked on several projects together over the years. Our design sensibilities are very similar. That said, Susanna has her own style, to say the least.

Susanna has great instincts, impeccable taste, and a background in interior design. She worked with me for three years and is a freelance writer and photo stylist for shelter magazines. What's more, she had a clear vision for the house. Having stayed at Little Bay for all those years, she knew just what needed to be done. That removed a lot of the guesswork from the equation. So it wasn't just fun but also surprisingly easy.

The two-story house is in the traditional Bahamian style, which means that almost all of the interior walls are white. Because of the humidity, they have to be completely repainted every year. The walls that aren't painted white are natural wood paneling, the appearance of which I really like. They look good and have an easier upkeep, which absolutely must be a primary consideration when designing any vacation house. Ski lodges, desert houses, and beach houses all have their own environmental challenges. For instance, people always ask how we got furniture over to the island. It's not easy. It all has to be shipped to Florida and then shipped to the island on a container—yet another thing to take into consideration when making decisions.

Aesthetics cannot be the only concern. Good design takes all the elements into account. Our starting point was Susanna's love of the water. It was always on our mind as we designed the space. And how could it not be? The ocean is literally all around.

For practicality's sake, we furnished the living room with washable slipcovers on the sofas and striped cotton rugs that can be easily cleaned and washed. They look and feel terrific in that space, and the inevitable encounters with dirt and sand don't create lasting problems.

The dining room table is a perfect example of the melding of form and function necessary in almost any vacation house. It is ivory lacquer faux bamboo with a laminate top. The seats of the chairs are ivory faux patent leather. A lot of thought went into selecting these pieces, not only for their look but also taking into account their durability.

For all these little consolations and compromises, their house has far more than a veneer of sophistication. Susanna and I found the fabulous 1960s Hollywood Regency ivory lacquer coffee table at a vintage shop in Palm Beach. I think of it as the centerpiece of the living room.

The custom Manhattan tables from my collection look perfect on either side of the sofa. They're upholstered in raffia, which, along with the caned dining chairs, pays homage to traditional British Colonial island design.

Susanna and Palmer have truly refined taste, which extends to their art. Over the sofa, we hung a wonderful black-and-white photograph by John Gynell that they purchased on the island at the Princess Street Gallery. Custom lampshades and pillows add polish to the living room and every other room in the house.

The faux-bamboo chandelier was one Susanna found in Palm Beach. Though they are typically painted white, the natural finish of this one creates an unexpected contrast with all the white slipcovers and the dining table. It was a great discovery.

Ocean colors are accents everywhere throughout the house. We accessorized with turquoise and deep blues, as well as pops of pinks and yellows in pillows and rugs. Susanna and I are both drawn to beautiful, shimmering glass as well as natural elements, like the shells her family collects from area beaches.

Susanna isn't afraid of whimsical touches, which makes decorating with her such a pleasure. Nowhere is her openness and great eye for unconventional style more apparent than in her collection of buoy sculptures in the shapes of carved faces, made by a local artist.

Ultimately, the setting is what it's all about. Boating to nearby islands for picnics. Swimming and snorkeling. Lunches at Sip Sip, one of their favorite spots for a long, leisurely midday meal. Drinks at The Landing, with its Hemingway-esque charm. Dinner at Dunmore Beach Club. And most of all, sunsets on the veranda at Little Bay.

PRECEDING PAGES:
Little Bay is a typical Bahamian cottage facing the bay.

ABOVE AND OPPOSITE:
Bright white walls and a black-and-white print by John B. Gynell are featured in the living/dining room, along with a vintage Hollywood Regency coffee table.

ABOVE:
The family collects sand dollars
from nearby beaches.

OPPOSITE:
The master bedroom with crisp,
white linen drapery and bedding,
accentuated by vintage black-
and-white photographs of
Harbour Island.

OPPOSITE:
The upstairs bedrooms all have
natural wood-paneled walls
that add warmth. Eliza enjoys
reading in her room.

ABOVE:

Susanna loves sunsets
on the veranda.

Artist's Aerie

Linda Bacon has been one of my best friends since our shared childhood growing up in small-town Texas. She is a brilliantly talented and well-regarded photorealist painter living in Marin County with her husband, Charles, a fellow Texan. Linda moved to San Francisco in 1966. She fell in love with California and never looked back. Charles' story is much the same. When they met and fell in love, Charles already had a home in Marin, where they lived for many years.

In 2000, they began looking for a house where Linda could have her studio at home, and they found a 1938 Gardner Dailey house located on the crest of a hill. Credited with bringing modernist design to California, Dailey is a well-known architect who, among other projects, designed the Coral Casino in Santa Barbara. I looked at the house online after Linda called to tell me about it. "Do whatever you have to do to buy this house," I told her. It has an incredible provenance, views of Mount Tamalpais and the Golden Gate Bridge, and it was built in a time period I love.

Even the grounds of the house have a significant history. They were designed by Thomas Church, one of the most influential landscape architects of the twentieth century, who frequently worked with Dailey when both were at the height of their careers.

The house looks as though it could have been designed by a forward-thinking architect today, and the influence of Dailey's work is still felt in much of today's architecture. Because the house was built in 1938, and since I have an affinity for antiques from the late 1930s and 1940s, I suggested that we acquire, through buying trips to Paris and New York, furnishings that would give the impression of having been collected from the time of the house's construction until the present day.

As is typical of Gardner Dailey houses, the entrance is a long, wide gallery with a glass wall looking out onto the view. On the other wall, Linda and Charles display her art as well as works by some of their favorite artists.

I love everything about the living room: the game table surrounded by leather upholstered Ruhlmann chairs, the Porteneuve-style console behind the sofa with red cloisonné lamps, and a late-Deco marquetry commode.

One of Linda's paintings, *Bingo*, hangs over the fireplace, which is surrounded by custom bookcases designed by architect Kathy Strauss. Strauss was brought on by Linda and Charles to help adapt the house to their needs, and she did such careful and admirable work throughout, keeping architectural elements consistent and scrupulously considering Dailey's principles at every turn.

The seating area in front of the windows is precisely the kind of cozy, high-style setting I try to create in all my designs. Lit by a Fontana Arte lamp, this spot is furnished with a comfortable silk velvet Paris Banquette, a round nickel-and-mirrored 1940s coffee table, and chairs attributed to Jean Rothschild. The effect is that of a room within a room.

The final touch in the living room is a pair of Rothschild Club Chairs from my collection. Inspired and named for the work of designer Jean Rothschild, they are upholstered in stark black cowhide welted in white leather and are incredibly bold and handsome in that setting.

There's not a bad seat in this room, and I mean that in both senses. Sitting at the game table facing the interior of the house, one sees a fabulous staircase typical of Gardner Dailey's design from that period. From the Rothschild Chairs, one can take in some of the best views of Mount Tamalpais in all of Marin County.

Dailey referred to his dining rooms as "garden rooms" because they were often surrounded on three sides by windows and felt like a combination of indoors and outdoors. This one is in that very style and overlooks the Thomas Church gardens. Linda found the Deco chandelier, and I found another set of Ruhlmann chairs and an elegant late-Deco rosewood buffet. The lighted cove at the top of the dining room ceiling is another Dailey signature.

Linda's artist studio is just off the kitchen on the first floor of the house and looks out onto the swimming pool. She has a vast collection of antique and vintage toys and a variety of other objects that inspire her colorful work.

The master bedroom has the same garden view as the dining room below and has the same basic design with windows on three sides. It is truly like being in a tree house. We kept the room very simple with low bookcases beneath the windows

and low late-Deco chairs in the corners. The leather and merisier headboard was custom made, and Linda found small, mirrored bedside tables that fit the space.

Charles and Linda love to entertain, and the house lends itself beautifully to that purpose. Their large guesthouse, called "the bunkhouse," is completely disconnected from the main house, which means that they can easily host friends for overnight stays. The list of people who have stayed there runs the gamut— artists, musicians, and actors. Linda and Charles are always looking for a reason to celebrate, and their parties are favorites of mine. When I'm in town, they usually give a dinner party for Jim and me, where we inevitably meet a cast of the most interesting characters.

ABOVE:
A view of the trademark Gardner
Dailey staircase and a pair
of Rothschild Chairs in black
cowhide with white leather welt.

OPPOSITE:
One of Linda's paintings, *Bingo*,
hangs over the living room
fireplace.

PRECEDING PAGES:
Every piece in the living room takes its cues from the architecture of the late 1930s.

RIGHT:
A secondary seating area looks out onto Mount Tamalpais.

Lake House Charm

Betty Ray and Bobby Dohoney have been close friends, clients, and neighbors of ours for more than thirty years. They are such an engaging and unusual couple. She is a retired law professor; he is a retired judge, Civil War authority, and history buff with an admirable book collection. They both love travel and have been all over the world. The Dohoneys enjoy spending time together and have very similar taste, so it's always easy for them to make decisions about how they want to live their lives and how they want to decorate their houses.

We spent years decorating their primary residence. During that time they purchased a lake house on Lake Whitney that had long been in Betty Ray's family. The project took on an added significance when they decided it would become their primary residence at the time of their retirement. At that point, they knew the size of the house would have to be increased substantially. They brought on architect Don Young, who was under instructions to retain the old, small structure but to capture the views from their unique vantage on a point overlooking the lake. By the end of construction, the square footage of the house had nearly tripled, allowing for a floor plan that accommodates their children and grandchildren, who come frequently for weekend visits.

Their house is positioned in an ideal spot at the end of a private road. Gardening is a genuine passion for Betty Ray, and it shows in the grounds of the property, where the landscaping is beautifully manicured. A pair of exotic palms flanks the covered entrance.

The entry hall is painted a soft, golden yellow. Faux-parquet painted and stained wood floors create visual interest, lend old-world charm, and make a great first impression that draws you into the space. Along with Majolica parrots from

Betty Ray's extensive Majolica bird collection, a bright red Murano glass lamp sits on a nineteenth-century painted French console I found in Paris.

Off the entry, steps lead down into the vast living space, with a glass wall overlooking a grove of live oak trees, indigenous to the area and abundant on the property. Beyond them, the lake is visible. Doors open onto a large deck from which the breathtaking vista is even easier to enjoy.

The living room is inviting with its slipcovered sofas and comfortable chairs. In accessorizing, we selected grass-green Marbro Murano glass lamps, as well as a softly colored Oushak rug.

Adjacent to the living room, the dining room shares the same sensational view. The French table is nineteenth-century Louis XVI style with custom Antibes Chairs upholstered in faux suede for practicality. An amber Murano chandelier called the Elizabeth, from my furniture and lighting collection, adds brilliance and a reflective quality to the room.

A marble-topped baker's table near the window is absolutely charming. For that spot we found another grass green Marbro Murano lamp—this one in a fabulous column design—to which we added a custom shade, base, and finial. A collection of amber Murano glass sits atop the late-Deco buffet complementing the late nineteenth-century water-gilt mirror.

Rather than using drapery on the windows, Conrad woven shades were used in the main rooms. They are custom made in Asia and can require months to arrive. I would not be so patient—nor would my clients—but for the fact that they last forever and let in just enough light to create an ethereal glow when closed.

A long hallway lined with books leads to the master bedroom, which has its own spectacular lake views. Drawing our cues from the blues of the water and the green live oaks just outside, we decided to paint the room in Donald Kaufman #25—a favorite color of mine, which I think of as pond green. The upholstered ivory headboard in reverse French welt pops against the wall color, as does the white quilt at the end of the bed, made by Betty Ray, a testament to her patience, skill, and fine taste.

Stacks of photo albums sit at the foot of the bed on a hand-forged iron bench, upholstered in raffia, that I found in Paris. I like the way the Dohoneys' books of photographs look there, reminders of the things that matter most in the world to them—their family and adventures. The albums are so personal, which to me is the secret of a successfully designed room.

PRECEEDING PAGE:
The entry has painted floors and
a nineteenth-century console

ABOVE:
A Majolica bird from Betty Ray's
collection.

OPPOSITE:
The expansive living room
overlooks the lake and a large
oak tree. A Côte d'Azur ebonized
and gold leaf coffee table sits
at the center of the room.
Vintage Murano lamps in peridot
by Marbro flank the sofa.

FLAGSTAFF

Equestrian Compound

The first project I did for Joann and Paul Delaney was their horse ranch just outside Flagstaff, Arizona. They contacted me after reading a magazine article about a house I did in Bachelor Gulch, Colorado, and invited me to look at their new house. Construction had just been concluded.

I learned in our first meeting that Joann and Paul are true equestrians, who both ride every day. They are also avid fox hunters, and have many horses and keep them not only on this property but also on another ranch nearby, where they keep their hunting dogs as well.

Their property is a vast compound with a horse barn and guest cottages. When I first saw what they had built, I was impressed that the architect, Mark Candelaria, used indigenous stone and wood in the construction. The Delaneys told me they loved French antiques with simple, clean lines, and were attracted to something I'd said in the magazine article about using antiques in every room. They weren't interested in having a house that looked like a lovely hotel suite. They wanted it to be personal. Since my mantra is "We don't want your house to look like a hotel," I knew we would get along swimmingly.

There are three main hallways: an entry hall, a central gallery, and another hallway leading into the living room, a beautifully scaled, spacious room with several seating areas. A pair of consoles I found in New York flanks a large French iron mirror in the hall leading to the living room. They were a great find and a perfect aesthetic for the look of the house.

At one end of the living room is a fireplace with a comfortable sofa and chairs placed to enjoy the fire. A dry bar sits nearby for use when entertaining guests. At the opposite end of the room, a seating area affords space for lounging

and watching television. The Delaneys' collection of Russian Impressionist art is on display throughout the house, and a particularly special grouping hangs over the sofa in this area.

Because all the other colors in the house were warm, we decided to paint the dining room a soft French blue. I found an extremely large fumé-colored oval Murano chandelier in Paris along with a French 1940s burled fruitwood buffet with bleached, hand-carved wood panels. An over-mantel etched mirror hangs above the buffet, adding sparkle and another dimension to the room. At the far end of the

An unusual chandelier of iron and original parchment from the 1930s hangs over a merisier game table in the hearth room.

dining room, we created a much more intimate setting: a square rock maple table with two chairs and beautiful views to the grounds outside, for dining à deux.

Down the central hallway is the kitchen. An antique parchment-and-iron chandelier I found in Paris hangs over the large kitchen island. Many of my clients collect glass, but Joann has a real affinity and a great eye for ceramics as well. Many of them are on display in the kitchen and hearth room, which is the name Joann and Paul gave to the space off the kitchen. That space is used as another casual dining area, with its French 1940s breakfast table in merisier and four ebonized French dining chairs upholstered in white cowhide. Another hand-forged iron chandelier, constructed of the inner workings of antique industrial machinery, hangs overhead. As unique as it is, it's not terribly unusual to find an antique iron chandelier in good condition. It was, however, somewhat incredible to find the original parchment shades perfectly intact. They had to be shipped over in a container of many antiques, and I held my breath until they arrived safely in the States.

Upstairs, the first room one reaches is the small library and sitting room, with an exquisite 1950s Italian credenza of rosewood and sycamore. This room is a passage leading into the master bedroom, which is spacious with beautiful views of the grounds. An inviting seating area surrounds the fireplace, with an iconic Robsjohn-Gibbings coffee table and a pair of vintage 1960s Hollywood Regency upholstered chairs. The walls are a soothing shade of Italian olive green. Another piece of Russian Impressionist art hangs over the mantel. Cenedese glass in a pale greenish gold complements this tableau.

Off the master bath is an old-school sleeping porch with just enough space for a comfortable custom bed and two custom bedside tables. It is rustic and romantic. Since summers in Flagstaff are cool, Joann and Paul are drawn to this space—with windows on three sides—because it is so warm and sunny.

There are four outdoor areas for entertaining, all with custom-designed French garden furniture. I adore French garden furniture from the 1940s. It has become very difficult to find, so we very often reproduce it, as we did for the Delaneys.

Paul and Joann love spending time outdoors at their amazing Flagstaff property. That's really what it's all about in their equestrian compound—the natural environment and enjoying the animals that bring them such pleasure, including their three house dogs, who are delightful and ever present. Of course, in Arizona, the setting is lovely in the spring and summer. In the winter months, however, the weather can become extreme with lots of snow, so it's essential that the indoors offers maximum coziness, comfort, and pleasure.

ABOVE:

A 1940s French oak credenza and triptych mirror by Brot with a blue Odegard rug.

OPPOSITE:

A Dino Martens lamp sits on one of a pair of unusual nineteenth-century consoles found in New York in a side entry hall leading to the spacious living room.

PRECEEDING PAGES:
A soothing yellow-green custom
wall color creates a warm
backdrop for the sofas and
chairs in the master bedroom.
The painting over the mantel is
another from their collection of
Russian Impressionist works.

OPPOSITE:
A romantic and inviting sleeping
porch off the master bath.

Sophisticated Mountain Hideaway

About seven years ago, two days after Christmas, Paul Delaney phoned from London. He and Joann had just left Telluride, where they had found a three-story townhouse they were interested in buying. Situated at the base of the mountain, it was close to the ski gondolas and to downtown. The real draw of the property was the fact that, due to restrictions, their view could never be obstructed.

The Delaneys loved the location, but they were concerned about the interior finish-out. They wanted to be certain I thought it would be a successful project. Joann and Paul knew that I knew exactly what they would want, having done their home in Flagstaff several years before. I got on a plane the next day to see the townhouse and meet with their contractor. When Paul called later that evening, I told him that, while I thought the house could be made into something wonderful, the process would be daunting. Paul and Joann were undeterred and decided to move forward, so the work began.

Telluride is a charming mining town that sits in a box canyon. The mountain views of Beaver Pond and the Bridal Veil Falls there are among the most dramatic in the entire state. And they are both visible from the Delaneys' property.

The Delaneys have been going to Telluride for many years with their family. They love the summer months in particular for hiking, biking, and horseback riding, as they are true equestrians. It is a convenient getaway, because it is also the closest ski resort to their primary residence in Flagstaff.

An entry on the first floor has a handsome Directoire-style commode combined with a mirror, a sculpture, and bronze lamp. As it happened, I had just purchased the commode in Paris, and it was already in my showroom. It was perfect for the space. The Duchess Mirror is from my collection, and the bronze lamp is French from the 1970s. The stone sculpture, by an unidentified artist, was also purchased in Paris.

The two bedrooms on the first level presented design challenges because of their long, narrow, hall-like architecture. My goal was to make the rooms look inviting and cozy for cool Colorado nights and snowy winter days. I found the solution when I decided to fabric the walls with two toiles: one more masculine for the Delaneys' two sons, Ian and Will, and the other more feminine for their daughter, Nora. This approach resolved every issue the rooms presented, covering up a multitude of sins. It wasn't easy convincing Joann and Paul, who are not big fans of prints, but they finally agreed. I knew it would achieve the desired effect. And it had the secondary benefit of bringing a feeling of warmth into the space and of making the rooms less imposing.

In the more masculine space, we utilized brown-and-ivory toile, with oxblood accents. A Napoleon III mirror breaks up the long wall and creates the impression of having a window in that space.

The toile in Nora's room is a feminine blue-and-gold pattern. We designed a bed treatment from the same fabric because I firmly believe that when you use toile, you should really use it!

The second floor consists of the living room, dining room, and kitchen. The stunning Rocky Mountain views are visible from each space.

It was understood from the start that the views were the primary feature. I'm never a fan of fussy interiors, but in the case of this property we were careful to keep things particularly edited so as not to clash or compete with the amazing vistas. The existing walls were a soft, golden-ivory plaster. We kept them as they were and used drapery in a complementary sand color. We used a white cowhide on the soft wall-to-wall carpet. The seating area comprises French 1940s bergères upholstered in sage-green velvet and a Gigi Chair and ottoman from my furniture collection, upholstered in black cowhide. The terrace off the living room is wonderful for lunch or cocktails at dusk, or watching the moonrise over the mountains.

The dining room has a custom Oliver Table in merisier with Antibes Chairs in walnut with striped leather, and a fabulous 1930s fumé-colored Murano chandelier is stylish and sophisticated. As a counterpoint to the glass, we used ceramics on the table and ceramic lamps on the cerused oak French buffet. A water-gilt Napoleon III mirror reflects the chandelier.

The entire third floor is the master suite. The bedroom is spacious, with the same spectacular mountain views as the living room, plus a large seating area where Joann and Paul can enjoy privacy away from the rest of the household. Joann had seen the bed, which I had used in another mountain project in this book, in a magazine. It made perfect sense in this space as in the other, because of the high ceilings. Everything in the seating area, except for the mirror, is French 1940s, with Jacques Adnet bergères on unusual sycamore bases. The bedside tables are mid-century American.

Joann tells me each time she returns from Telluride how she adores the townhouse. "It's like being in a New York apartment," she says, "but with amazing Telluride views."

PRECEDING PAGES:
The warm and sophisticated interior is a dramatic contrast to the mountain views beyond. A pair of antique bergères are upholstered in sage velvet. The Gigi Chair and Ottoman are upholstered in black cowhide.

OPPOSITE:
The fumé-colored 1930s Murano chandelier is reflected in a water-gilt Napoleon III mirror. The credenza is French oak from the 1940s, and the table and chairs are from my collection.

ABOVE:
The kitchen has breathtaking mountain views.

ABOVE:

A pair of 1950s ebonized sycamore commodes with vintage Murano glass lamps flanks the Pierre Deux bed.

OPPOSITE:

A cozy seating area with Jacques Adnet bergères with sycamore bases on either side of a Hadley sofa. Turquoise accents are unexpected against the warm palette of the room.